HOW TO WIN THE LOTTERY

The Essential Guide

Dr. M. Harding, Ph.D.

MAK Books

First published in Great Britain in 1996 by MAK Books
an imprint of MAK Publishing
PO Box 72, Oxford OX1 5QB, U.K.

ISBN 0 9527804 0 2

Printed in Great Britain by Uniprint, Oxford

CONTENTS

PREFACE

Failing to achieve our objectives is often put down to bad luck which is seen as something out of our control. One of the best descriptions of luck, however, is: "preparation meeting the moment of opportunity". It is this preparation that can make the difference between being 'lucky' or 'unlucky'.

The objective of this book is purely to show you how to improve your chances in the lottery. It is not to endorse lottery in general, any lottery organisation or any charitable cause benefiting from this game. The judgement of all moral, ethical or other issues related to playing lottery is left to the reader. The author would, however, like to emphasise both responsible playing and the curbing of under age playing.

Dr. M. Harding

1

BACKGROUND

Winning in a lottery £1 million, £5 million, £10 million or even more can only be described as a dream come true. The possibility of becoming an instant millionaire has universal appeal. The fact that anyone can win, regardless of their background, has made playing lottery so popular.

You might prefer there to be a lot of smaller prizes rather than one big payout - the **jackpot**. It is, however, the big prizes that generate the buzz. The bigger the jackpot, the more people play, increasing its size even further. For example, in the U.S.A. there are massive jackpots in excess of $100 million.

Lottery is not a new phenomenon. The first public lotteries can be traced back to Roman times and throughout history they have been used to raise money, either for general revenue or for specific purposes. In Britain, for example, Westminster Bridge (1739) was built and what became the British Museum (1753) established with the funds from a national lottery. The modern version of lottery emerged in the U.S.A. in the 60's. With its heavy promotion in the media, it quickly became part of everyday life, and is now found all over the world.

There is a lottery in every European country, in most states of the U.S.A., in the former Soviet Union, and in Australia, New Zealand and Israel.

Lotteries can be divided into three main types. In the classic **lotto games** usually six numbers are chosen from many **options**. The **numbers games**, in which three or four numbers are chosen, are similar to lotto but with smaller prizes. In the **instant win** or **scratch card games** the player can tell from the ticket whether or not a prize, which is typically small, has been won. In this book we concentrate on the lotto game only and the names lotto and lottery are used interchangeably.

2

LOTTO GAME

In the lotto game players select their own numbers from an option of between 44 and 54 numbers. Usually six numbers count as one **entry**. The aim is for the player to match his/her own numbers with a set of six numbers **drawn** by the lottery organiser. Prizes are given for three, four, five and six correct numbers. A **bonus number**, which is an extra number drawn in addition to the six draw numbers, can be included to create another prize. In Britain, for example, the second prize is given for five correct numbers plus the bonus number.

The lotto prizes are made up of the players' contributions to the **prize pool** minus the organiser's expenses and usually a donation to good causes. The smallest prize, say for three correct numbers, is often a fixed one. Other prize values are a predetermined percentage of the total prize pool, and depend on the number of people playing. The more players there are, the bigger the prizes are too. The actual prizes the winners get do not, however, increase in proportion to the number of players. This is because there is also an increase in the number of winners at the same time.

As the selection of the lottery numbers is made from a large option, there is a good chance that the jackpot is not won, and is carried forward to the next draw. This, a so-called **rollover**, can take place several times in consecutive draws. If there is no limit to the number of rollovers, huge jackpots can be created.

3

CHANCES OF WINNING

Lottery is a game of chance. If you play a 6/49 game, which is henceforward used in this book as a reference game, the chances of winning the jackpot are one in 13,983,816 ~14 million (see Appendix A). The chances of winning other prizes are one in:

2,330,636	- five numbers + the bonus number;
54,201	- five numbers;
1,032	- four numbers;
56.7	- three numbers;
53.7	- any prize.

The way these figures are calculated is shown in Appendix B.

The chances of winning in the lottery are small compared with, for example, those in betting on horses. Nonetheless, if you play one entry weekly you should win at least a small prize once a year. Furthermore, as there are one or more winners of the jackpot almost weekly, there is no reason why it could not be you.

The lottery organisers do their utmost to ensure that the numbers are **drawn randomly**. This means that each number has the same **probability** (chance) of being drawn. Number 11, for instance, is as likely to come up as number 35. In addition, each draw is independent, and does not depend on previous draws or affect any future draw. Under these conditions, it seems that there is very little you can do to improve your chances of winning. There are, however, a number of things that you can do to improve your game. Before going into such details, let us first clarify some basic features of the lotto game.

Often the word **permutation** is used in the context of lotteries. Permutating lottery numbers simply means rearranging them in a different order. As the order of the numbers does not matter in most lotto games, the use of the term permutation is misleading. Instead, what we need to know, in order to calculate the chances of winning, is the number of **combinations**. Combinations are sets of numbers that can be made from a larger set. For example, a set of three numbers {5,9,14} has: one three-number combination {5,9,14}; three two-number combinations {5,9}, {5,14}, {9,14}; and three one-number combinations {5}, {9}, {14}. As calculated in Appendix A, the number of six-number combinations in a 6/49 game is almost 14 million. Thus, your chances of winning the jackpot with one entry are one in 14 million.

Theoretically, all the combinations in the lotto game are as likely, although no six consecutive numbers have ever been known to come up in a draw. To explain this and other features of the lotto game, knowledge of the behaviour of **random numbers** can be very useful. One of the applications is the elimination of unlikely combinations. Some of the unlikeliest are intuitively recognised by most but not all of us. For instance, thousands of people still hope to be the only ones to win the jackpot with numbers 1 to 6. There are, however, many risks involved in evaluating likely combinations without a proper understanding of random processes in lottery draws. Every week, self-appointed lottery 'experts' impose their views and censorship on their family members' combinations. There is the true story of a man who did not believe that the combination his family obtained with a kids' toy lottery machine was likely to come up. Had he known more about the behaviour of lottery numbers, he would not have thrown away the numbers that turned out to be that week's jackpot combination. The poor man's only defence is that this book was not yet available at the time!

Sometimes, you may have one or more numbers in your entry that appear to be very 'close' to a particular draw number. Say, the draw number was 2 but you had number 3. It can be disappointing to 'just miss' a prize, all the more so if it was the jackpot - but it is an illusion that a lottery number can be 'close'. There is no such thing. Unless the numbers are on a revolving board binding them together, which is unlikely for a lottery draw, all the numbers are equally 'close' to each other. Thus, numbers 15 and 45 are as 'close' to number 2 as number 3 is.

A much overlooked aspect of playing lottery is sharing the jackpot prize with others who have the same combination. For every 30 million players in a 6/49 game you would expect to have a couple of winning tickets. You may now think that winning even a share of the jackpot would make you seriously rich. That is not necessarily the case, particularly in lotto games which do not have a **quick pick** option (also known by other names such as Lucky Dip). This is a terminal system, which gives the players their own individual sets of randomly generated numbers. In games without the quick pick, there are a lot of draws where the jackpot is either shared with a large number of people or it is rolled over without there being a single winner. The reason is that players tend to choose similar combinations. The result is twofold. There are multiple winners, while a large number of combinations remain unplayed. As an example, the U.K. National Lottery had in the 9th week of its operation a rollover jackpot of £19 million. After the initial elation, the winners' joy soon turned sour when they learned that there were altogether 133 winning tickets and the once in a lifetime chance of a big win was lost! This is not a one-off event. In week 70 there were 57 winning tickets to share a jackpot of £8.3 million.

In the next few chapters, we will look into how to select lottery numbers that have a better chance of winning, and a smaller chance of being shared by a lot of other players.

4

RANDOM SELECTIONS

Selecting your numbers at random is the closest method to the actual lottery draw. It may lack the mystique of some other methods but is, nevertheless, the key method of winning a lottery. This is not to say that you cannot win using something else, but a random selection offers you unparalleled advantages. Firstly, it utilises the whole spectrum of the available combinations. It has been estimated that up to 25% of all combinations are regularly left unselected by the players. Secondly, numbers chosen at random are less likely to be picked by many other players, reducing the risk of having to share the prizes. The introduction of the quick pick lottery terminals has made it much easier to play with random numbers.

If there is no quick pick available in your lotto game or, like many of us, you want to add the personal touch to your entry, you can generate random numbers yourself. Choosing lottery numbers at random appears to be extremely easy and, thus, is often seen as the lazy individual's way of playing. Many people fill in their coupons in a hurry at the lottery outlets. When asked how they chose the numbers the casual answer is often, "I just picked them at random". This is not necessarily the case. Those who tick their coupons 'at random' are very unlikely to end up with essentially a random selection of numbers. This is prevented by the very nature of our thinking processes. We are programmed to make logical connections. Thus, it is very difficult to choose numbers independent of each other. Furthermore, even the way we see the coupon affects the selection. The visual illusion that the area at the top of the coupon for the small numbers appears to be bigger than the area for the large numbers distorts our selection.

To select your random numbers you do not need fancy computer programmes or other devices. All you need to do is to write all the lottery numbers on separate pieces of paper, put them in a box, and draw your numbers from it.

Although lacking in mystique, random selection can be made fun and many imaginative people have devised some really interesting ways of choosing their numbers. One man marked the lottery numbers on the tyre of his motor-bike. He then drove, and stopped at random to pick the number that was closest to the road. Another blew up balloons, marked them with lottery numbers, and let his dog loose to burst them. The first six burst ones produced his combination. You can use your telephone directory by opening it randomly and, without looking, put your finger somewhere on the page. The house number that you chance upon can be used. If it is not one of the lottery numbers, you can still use it. Number 365 produces, for example, numbers 36, 35, and 14 (=3+6+5). You can also note down numbers that randomly appear around you, such as bus numbers, numbers on the side of vans, etc. - in fact any number that for some reason attracts your attention.

Without being overzealous, a certain amount of care should be taken when generating random numbers. To obtain true random numbers, the method used has to be totally independent of outside influence be it your mind, skill or any feature arising from the method itself. Many selections that appear to be random ones are not that at all. We already pointed out the method of ticking the lottery coupons. Putting a piece of paper containing all the lottery numbers on a dart board and then throwing darts to choose numbers is not, strictly speaking, a random selection either. This is because the thrower's skill or lack of it is involved in the selection. Sometimes it is difficult to see whether the system itself is at fault. You may use some kind of device, equipment or a computer programme which itself has an inbuilt **bias** toward certain numbers. This may be very difficult to detect.

Once you have selected your numbers, the question arises as to whether or not to change them from draw to draw. This problem remains largely unresolved. It can be argued that by changing your combination you may be throwing away the very one that could have won you the jackpot at a later date. Indeed, there are winners who have kept the same numbers for a very long time, winning in the end. On the other hand, a particular combination that you have kept from draw to draw may not come up in your lifetime. Furthermore, keeping the numbers the same continuously, makes some people anxious not to miss a single draw in case it will be, at long last, the lucky one. The time to review your combination is, at least, when you win some of the prizes. The better the prize you win, the less likely you are to win again with that combination.

In the next chapter we will look at some alternative methods of choosing lottery numbers and at how to improve your existing method.

5

ALTERNATIVE SELECTIONS

If, at present, you use some numbers that you regard as precious or lucky, do not despair. You can, by all means, continue using them. While random numbers automatically produce combinations with good chances of winning, your entry can be made as good by using the knowledge of the behaviour of random numbers.

It is understandable if you have some kind of attachment to special numbers which add extra mystique to playing lottery. It may also give a feeling of personal involvement and even control over the draw. This is harmless as long as we do not lose touch with reality.

DATES AS LOTTERY NUMBERS

There are literally thousands and thousands of methods people use to choose their lottery numbers. However, one method is more common than any other. This is the use of dates of birthdays, anniversaries or other meaningful events. Indeed, jackpots have been won with such dates. As the numbers in lottery are randomly drawn, there is no reason why your dates would not come up. However, as the dates produce numbers 1 to 31 and the months 1 to 12, your combination is bound to be heavily weighed towards these low numbers. Thus, a large proportion of available numbers becomes underrepresented. Furthermore, due to the popularity of dates in the selection of lottery numbers, you are likely to share any possible prize with many people with the same entry.

The sets of random numbers have many **statistical characteristics** that can be used to improve combinations. One of these features is the **sum of the numbers** within the entry. In the 6/49 game, both the smallest sum of 21 and the largest sum of 279 are produced by only one corresponding combination. On the other hand, the average sum of 150 can be produced by a total of 165,772 combinations. The following table shows the percentage of all combinations within given ranges of sums.

Sum range	Combinations
140 - 160	24.5%
130-139 & 161-170	21.4%
120-129 & 171-180	18.0%
110-119 & 181-190	13.8%
100-109 & 191-200	9.7%
90-99 & 201-210	6.2%

It appears that if the sum of your numbers is very small, in addition to there being the risk of prize sharing, your combination is not likely to come up at all. For example, using date numbers 1 to 31 yields an average sum of 96. This represents only 46,253 combinations. On the other hand, if all your numbers are excessively high, your chances are no better. Thus, you would be better advised to adjust the sum of the numbers in your entry if it is below 100 or over 200. Bearing in mind that people tend to choose low numbers, setting your sum in the region of 130-180 would be more advisable.

By all means, use some of your dates but sparingly, particularly numbers 12 and under, and include a couple or more numbers over 31 in your combination. Furthermore, try to keep a balance between the **odd** and the **even numbers**. With just simple measures you can significantly improve your entry.

SEQUENCES

Sequences are sets of numbers that have been arranged systematically, each number depending on the previous one. Sequences come in many forms. They can be consecutive numbers, every second, third, fourth, etc., or numbers obtained by adding or multiplying. The following are examples of some of the possible lottery sequences:

31, 32, 33, 34, 35, 36 - consecutive
17, 23, 29, 35, 41, 47 - every sixth
3, 6, 9, 15, 24, 39 - previous added
18, 19, 28, 29, 38, 39 - every fifth twin

Forming perfect sequences is against the characteristics of random numbers and only parts of sequences appear regularly in lottery draws. The mathematical probability of different sequences can be readily calculated. For example, two consecutive numbers called **twins**, such as 18 and 19, can be expected to come up in the 6/49 game in 51.3% of the draws. Thus, it does not matter whether you have twins or not in your combination, your chances of winning are the same. On the other hand, the probability of three consecutive numbers, **triplets**, is only 4.5%, and of four consecutive numbers a mere 0.3%. Five or six consecutive numbers are extremely remote: one every 336th and 317,814th draw, respectively. It is no surprise that six consecutive numbers have never been known to win. Other lotto game draws behave in the same way - the probability of twins in the 6/44 game is 55.9% and in the 6/54 game it is 47.4%. To make sure that your combination conforms to the type that regularly appears in draws, you would do best to avoid three or more consecutive numbers. The same applies to other sequences. Another reason for avoiding sequences is that a lot of people use them and you want to play against them.

DATES TO NUMBERS CONVERSION

As playing lottery with numbers generated from dates is such a fundamental method, let us look into some alternative ways of obtaining these numbers. A New York lottery winner used his birthday - April 1951. First he removed number 19 as it is common to everyone. This left him with numbers 4, 5 and 1 which have two-number combinations, 45, 41, 54, 51, 14, 15. He then replaced number 54, which was the largest available number in the game, with 5+1=6, giving the winning combination. The manipulation of dates allows you to produce numbers that, although still connected to the specific date, offer variety compared to simply using the date itself as a number. In the manipulation of dates, adding (e.g. 63 becomes 6+3=9) and reversing (e.g. 63 becomes 36) are useful tools. If your birthday does not feel lucky enough, you can use somebody else's birthday, whether it is a member of the family, a friend or a famous person. The so-called **soul path number** is generated from a birthday by adding all the numbers together. 14th October 1940 would give 1+4+1+0+1+9+4+0=20, from which 2+0=2 is the soul path number. As this number is always a single digit, and therefore in the range of numbers to be avoided, a multiple of it would be a better choice.

NAMES TO NUMBERS CONVERSION

In addition to dates, names play an important part in our lives. Special names can easily be converted into numbers using an **alphabet table**. To create a standard **three-row table**, write down numbers 0 to 9 and under them the letters of the alphabet in the following way:

1	2	3	4	5	6	7	8	9	0
a	b	c	d	e	f	g	h	i	j
k	l	m	n	o	p	q	r	s	t
u	v	w	x	y	z				

In the simplest form, you can use a twelve-letter name. For instance, Desperate Dan now translates into 459658105414. This gives us six numbers: 45, 96, 58, 10, 54, 14 of which in our 6/49 reference game the second, third and fifth numbers are out of the range. To these numbers we apply the **Reverse-Add-Reverse (R-A-R) technique**. Reversing 96 gives us 69, which is no better and we need to take the next step, and add 6 and 9 which is 15. In a similar way, reversing 58 it becomes 85 and we have to add 8 and 5 to give us 13. Finally, 54 reversed is 45, which we already have, and 4 is then added to 5 to give number 9. Thus, we have generated the combination: 9, 10, 13, 14, 15, 45. According to our guide lines this combination appears to have too many low numbers. It also includes a rare triplet with number 13 that many regard as an unlucky number. Let us now reverse it to obtain 31 and add numbers 9 and 10, for example, to 13 and 14, respectively, to give us 22 and 24. We now have a more balanced combination of: 14, 15, 22, 24, 31, 45 which still originates from the special name Desperate Dan.

If the name has more than twelve letters in it, you can either use only the first twelve or leave letters out, starting with the vowels, which are more common than the consonants in different names. Alternatively, you can initially form three- or even four-digit numbers, and then reduce the digits, as shown in the next chapter. The way you manipulate the translation of words into numbers gives your combination individuality. However, starting with a popular name may make it more difficult for you to be the only one with that particular combination.

The names to numbers conversion is also useful to those who believe that their dreams can have a meaning. For example, the dream of Having Dinner translates into 812947494458. Now 81 reversed is 18. Number 58 is first reversed to give 85, then added to make 13 and reversed again to produce 31. The other numbers are left as they are. Our dream has now produced the combination 18, 29, 31, 44, 47, 49.

The letters of the alphabet in the three-row table can also be arranged randomly, giving you the chance of having your own individual table. On the other hand, arranging the letters consecutively or randomly into a specific shape, such as a triangle, does not seem to offer any advantages. In such configurations, the letters of the alphabet are not evenly distributed, which may give rise to a bias towards some numbers.

Another method of creating an alphabet table is to allocate the letters randomly or consecutively between numbers 0 and 26 (number of letters in the English alphabet). However, this method does not seem to improve on the standard three-row table, but requires more optimising and balancing of the combinations.

FIGURES TO NUMBERS CONVERSION

Your special figure or shape can also be translated into lottery numbers. This conversion is done on a piece of squared paper, each square marked with a number between 0 and 9. The number of squares can be anything you like and the marking systematic or random. The figure or shape is then drawn onto these squares. Starting from one point, the line of the drawing is followed and the number on each square that the line crosses noted down. In our example, we obtain the numbers 176245937890022451. These can be divided into six three-digit numbers (176, 245, etc.). Then, by adding the last digit to the first two (17+6=23, 24+5=29, etc.), we can produce six two-digit lottery numbers 23, 29, 10, 89, 4, 46. The R-A-R method is then used to produce 17 from 89. As there are two numbers under 12, let us convert number 4 by adding it to, say, 10 which gives 14. Finally, let us reverse 23 to get 32 in order to have more numbers over 31 and to increase the number of even numbers. Our figure has then produced the combination 10, 14, 17, 29, 32, 46.

1	2	3	4	5	6	7	8	9	0
9	8	7	6	5	4	3	2	1	0
9	0	1	2	3	4	5	6	7	8
7	6	5	4	3	2	1	0	9	8
7	8	9	0	1	2	3	4	5	6
5	4	3	2	1	0	9	8	7	6
5	6	7	8	9	0	1	2	3	4
3	2	1	0	9	8	7	6	5	4

6

STATISTICAL APPROACH

The statistical approach simply means looking into a large amount of data in an attempt to find recognisable patterns, and to establish possible causes for these patterns. The applications range from customer buying trends to medical research. Therefore, it has appealed to many lottery enthusiasts as a tool for obtaining patterns also in lotteries. This could be, for example, the tendency for certain numbers to be drawn more frequently than others.

LOTTERY ALCHEMY

However attractive the prospect of finding a pattern in a lottery is, it has to be said clearly that this is an area only for **lottery alchemists**. You may remember the alchemists in the Middle Ages, who were determined, among other things, to create gold and silver from less valuable materials. In a similar way, there are those who desperately try to find a way of beating the lottery by studying data from past draws. Since drawing the lottery numbers is a random process, our modern day alchemists have not been able to find, nor will be able to find, patterns of any use. There is, however, one difference between the original and the new alchemists. Whereas the old ones did not achieve their goal, some of the modern ones at least make good money be selling their 'findings'.

There is no contradiction in using the knowledge of the behaviour of random numbers, as we did in the previous chapter, to improve your entries. The random draws have certain mathematical characteristics, which can be successfully exploited. This is not the case with data from past draws, which can not cast any new light on lotteries. There is no way you can predict the next draw numbers by studying the data from old draws. The only use for this data is for weeding out the past winning combinations. Although you are not likely to win with a combination which has already won a big prize, the chances that your entry is a past winning combination are extremely remote.

As there are quite a few misconceptions that may spoil your chances of winning, let us take a closer look at some of the most common ones.

BIAS

The aim of studying old lottery numbers is to detect a bias in the lottery machine. This bias would then manifest itself as a pattern in the draw results. The reason for the bias would be a small fault in the lottery machine or in the balls. Even the amount of paint used to number the different balls has been mentioned as a possible cause of bias by some extremists.

In **roulette**, bias is a problem even when there is a perfect wheel. This is because the wheel and the ball are operated manually. If it is done in a similar manner and using the same force every time, a certain area of the wheel is more likely to end up with the ball. For this reason, the croupier varies his/her handling of the wheel and ball to produce evenly distributed numbers.

Lottery machines are totally different as they, unlike roulette wheels, do not have the human input in generating numbers. Even the simplest lottery machines use sufficiently round balls, and mix them. During mixing, each ball interacts with considerable force with a large number of other balls which produces a random mix. After this, it does not matter how the balls are drawn, the result is a completely random combination. Furthermore, the machine, its parts and balls are changed frequently, invalidating past data. For convenience, options on lottery coupons are displayed in order.

However, because the draw is a random process there is no interrelation between the actual draw numbers and, as we already pointed out, they are all the same 'distance' from each other. This is the fact that makes pattern studies, which are based on the order of the numbers, clearly nonsense and a waste of time.

DISTRIBUTION OF NUMBERS

It may be confusing to see that during a fixed period of time there can be some numbers that have hardly appeared at all, while some others have come up many times and even in consecutive draws. Nonetheless, this is precisely how random numbers behave.

To demonstrate the behaviour of random numbers, let us start a hypothetical lottery game for the first time. In the first draw, six numbers come up. As the second draw is independent of the first one, all of the numbers are as likely to be drawn. Thus, new numbers or some of the ones that already appeared in the first draw will come up. In a similar way, the third draw will produce numbers that may not have been drawn before or have already been drawn once or even twice. After a while, a clear **distribution of numbers** starts to appear. Here, the bulk of the numbers has appeared a certain number of times, while a few numbers have appeared either rarely or very frequently. For example, already after 52 draws in the U.K. National Lottery one number had only been drawn once, while four numbers had already appeared as many as 10 times. In time, the distribution will develop further to have the characteristic shape of that particular game. This is all within the boundaries of random selections, and does not manifest any bias.

A further important feature is that within the distribution there takes place a **redistribution of numbers** all the time. This means that a number that has appeared the most frequently so far may or may not continue being the most regularly drawn in future draws. In a similar way, the least frequent number may or may not continue being the least frequent number. This irregular behaviour of lottery numbers, giving rise to the redistribution, invalidates all predictions of future draw numbers.

HIGH AND LOW FREQUENCY NUMBERS

A number which has appeared in several consecutive draws is often called a 'hot' number. All too often, it is wrongly concluded that such a number, or any other number that has been drawn many times in the past, is necessarily the one to come again. This also applies to a number that has not been drawn for ages. It may or may not be drawn. There is not such a thing as an 'overdue' number, or a 'cold' one, as it is often referred to. All numbers are drawn independent of their past history and there is nothing we can do about it.

COMPUTER ANALYSIS

The data analysis by some lottery alchemists goes much further than we have discussed so far. They even study, for example, the positions of the numbers in each individual draw and the occurrence of groups of two or more numbers, called clusters. As this is manually quite time-consuming, a number of computer programmes have emerged to do this.

As regards pattern recognition, a parallel has sometimes been drawn between lottery and the stock market, where computers are used to track down the share price movements on a large scale. However, we have to remember that although the stock exchange is the biggest gambling institution, there is a human influence somewhere along the line in the form of a manufacturer or supplier of a real product, or in the form of political decisions. Lottery, on the other hand, is just a repetition of random draws.

Computer software is, in general, a notoriously unreliable product. If the same number of faults occurred in household appliances, there would be a public outcry. The use of an expensive computer programme to track down non-existent patterns is, unfortunately, in itself a statement about the user. If you want to be a lottery winner, you should not start by losing money on lottery programmes. Naturally, prizes have been won, and will be won, by some of those who use computers. The marketeers of these programmes may attribute this to their products. The real reason is coincidence. Take enough people and statistically you will find prize winners. Furthermore, it is easy to make unsubstantiated claims. How do you check that Mr. or Mrs. Lottery-Winner from a far-away country really used a computer programme or any other lottery system?

7

LOTTERY SYSTEMS

FULL SYSTEMS

Most people play lottery with just one or two entries. If the entries are completely different (independent), still only six numbers are played at a time. More numbers can be played at the same time by overlapping entries to cover multiple combinations. To play more than six numbers, the entries required are (for the formula see Appendix A):

Numbers played	Entries required
6	1
7	7
8	28
9	84
10	210
11	462
12	924

It can be seen that increasing the numbers played quickly leads to a large number of combinations, and becomes very expensive.

The answer to the question of whether or not a system is worthwhile has to be no. You may think that wouldn't it be marvellous to be able to play seven, eight or more numbers rather than just six? Wouldn't it increase the chances of winning dramatically? On average, there is less than one (0.73) correct number in each independent entry. Say, you played two such entries, and were lucky to have one correct number in one entry and two in the other one. Playing a system, you could have combined the entries to produce three correct numbers, and to win a prize. Unfortunately, to produce the three correct numbers from your two entries, you would have had to play in practice 12 numbers that would have required 924 separate entries! Now you see what a large number of entries is required for such a small gain. In the light of this, the increased cost of playing seven or more numbers in a system is clearly not justified.

There is only one way to win the jackpot for sure and that is to play all the combinations available. This has been done several times. The most famous winner is an Australian, Peter Mandel, who has reputedly won the jackpot three times. His biggest jackpot was $27 million in the Virginia State Lottery. To produce the seven million combinations that were required for this 6/44 game, he was said to have employed 16 people, 20 computers and 16 laser printers. This is, however, not without a risk. As discussed earlier, the winning combination can sometimes be a very popular one and the jackpot is shared with a large number of people. Although other prizes are won at the same time, there is by no means any certainty that playing all the combinations will produce a net gain. In games with more options, and with a limit to the number of rollovers, the chances of a net gain are further reduced.

SHORT SYSTEMS

To reduce the high cost of playing full lottery systems, shorter versions have been introduced. They are simply off-cuts from the full systems and, not covering as many combinations, provide even less chance of winning. Short systems are marketed with the promise of improved chances of winning multiple small prizes. This is questionable in the light of the difficulty in winning these prizes even with a full system. The chances of winning small prizes are often described as 'guaranteed' if, and this is a big assumption, sufficiently many draw numbers are found among the numbers in the system. For example, the four-entry short wheel in Appendix C is 'guaranteed' to include at least one entry with five correct numbers, but only under the condition that all six draw numbers are found among these four entries. This is referred to as a 5 of 6 system. In a similar way, it is also a 4 of 5 and 3 of 4 system. Assumptions of six, five or four correct numbers within the system are completely unrealistic, and can be made about any system of multiple entries without it being anything special. Even two completely independent entries can be described as a 3 of 6 'system'. If multiple entries are played, a better option is to use randomly generated sets.

All lottery systems, but particularly the short ones which are more affordable than the long ones, carry the risk of encouraging players to invest more money in the game than they can afford.

Although it is not worth spending money on commercial lottery systems, nevertheless some players or syndicates may be tempted to do so. For this reason, a review of how these systems are devised is included in Appendix C.

8

FURTHER CONSIDERATIONS

OWNERSHIP OF LOTTERY TICKET

In many countries, the ownership of the lottery ticket is not registered and any person who has possession of a winning ticket can claim the prize. Thus, it is important to take care of your ticket to have it as proof for any prize claim. A policeman from Illinois reputedly found a friend's ticket on the floor, and refused to surrender it. He went on to win the jackpot, and kept the money.

Giving, or indeed receiving, lottery tickets as presents may sometimes cause problems. If you give a ticket that wins a big prize, it is up to the receiver to decide whether or not to share it. You may find that he/she decides that, although it would be only fair to split the money, your lifelong friendship is not worth it. If this happens, you not only lose a friend but also a lot of money that would otherwise have been yours. Receiving a winning ticket is the same problem, but the other way round.

UNCLAIMED PRIZES

Most lotteries impose a time limit for prize claims and a surprisingly large number of prizes remain unclaimed. For instance, in the U.K. National Lottery they amount to millions of pounds annually and not only include small ones, but big prizes of tens of thousands of pounds.

It is to be remembered that missing a prize claim can happen to anyone. One reason for this is that tickets get lost. As the tickets are quite small this is easy. Many a ticket has been ruined by keeping it in the pocket of the trousers or the shirt that has ended up in the washing machine. Another reason is that people do not check their numbers carefully enough against the draw numbers. Quite often we hear of people who have claimed a prize to discover that they have, in fact, won a bigger prize than they thought. Luckily, in such a situation, the ticket gets checked again. However, if the winner mistakenly assumes that not even the smallest prize is due, he/she simply throws the winning ticket away.

SYNDICATES

Joining a syndicate can improve your chances of winning by giving you a share of many entries. Therefore, syndicates have a wide appeal and a lot of people are regular members of one. However, joining a syndicate is not so straightforward and you should ask yourself:

> Can I trust the organiser? After collecting the money from the members does the organiser pocket it, or put it into the syndicate's lottery fund, as agreed? Do I know all the syndicate's combinations? If not, what prevents the organiser from keeping the winnings with the player whose numbers won? What stops the organiser running away with the winnings anyway?

Some people, unfortunately, are prepared to go to any length when large sums of money are at stake. To counteract some of the pitfalls of playing lottery in a syndicate, you should at least have a written agreement, which in some countries is a legal requirement for any claim to a share of the prize money. This agreement should cover, among other things, what happens if a player is unable to contribute for a particular week. Is he or she entitled to a share of the possible winnings? The level of investment and reinvestment from each player should also be agreed upon from the start, as well as each individual's requirements regarding publicity in the event of a big win.

Finally, you should ask yourself how you will feel if it is your combination that wins the jackpot. You may bitterly regret not playing on your own, and having to share your good luck with a syndicate, that may have a lot of members. The way around this problem is to use the syndicate's collective random numbers or to mix the numbers from different players. Then the winning would be a joint effort, and not riding on just one person's luck. Another, but more costly, way is to play the combination that you give to the syndicate on your own as well. This way, you would have to share only half of your winnings.

COMMERCIAL SYNDICATES

With commercial syndicates you have no control whatsoever. They combine all the pitfalls of a syndicate, but on a larger scale. There is a double lottery, firstly for winning and secondly for you getting your share of the winnings. The organiser does not risk anything, as you would pay for the overheads and profits. Often the organisers are based overseas, outside the player's own country's legislation.

WINNING THE BIG ONE

Winning the lottery can dramatically change your life. For most of the big prize winners, this is for the better and they lead very happy lives. Some money is spent on luxuries and the rest invested for financial security. These winners and their families are finally able to do all those things that they have previously only been dreaming of.

Unfortunately for some, the dream may turn sour due to insufficient planning at the time of winning. There can be court battles for money, unwelcome publicity, bad financial advice, etc. Winning the big one can put you on such a high that you might do something rash, and regret it later. It is not unknown for a winner to splash out too extravagantly, or to be too generous. A seaman from Toronto is said to have spent £250,000 in only 11 weeks. A large proportion of the money he gave away to friends and passers-by and, having given up his job, he ended up on the dole. It is also to be remembered that a sum that may initially seem enormous may not actually be so much when thinking of all the years ahead. In some lotteries, the big prize is not given as a lump sum, but as an annuity spread over a number of years.

Many lottery organisations provide their winners with expert advice on a range of subjects, including how to handle the money. This service is worthwhile having.

RESPONSIBLE PLAYING

Playing lottery should be for entertainment only. IT IS NOT AN ANSWER TO FINANCIAL PROBLEMS! If you have been unfortunate enough to lose more money in the lottery than you can afford, there is no way you can recover it by continuing to play, even by increasing the stakes. Under no circumstances should you embark on this road. It is destined to fail. If you feel that you have to have one more go, even when you know that you should not, you have a problem. You need to recognise it, and to seek help in time. There are examples of people who have lost their savings, houses and partners through gambling in lotteries. Although this problem is more associated with instant lotteries, the lotto game has its risks too.

Luckily, out of the millions and millions of lottery players, only a small fraction play above their means. The purpose of this book has been throughout to show you how to improve your chances in the lottery, and not how to spend more money on it. By following our guidelines, you can improve your chances without increasing your stake. Be aware also of the false hopes that lottery systems, computer programmes and commercial syndicates can create. Play lotteries responsibly - it affects not only you but also your nearest and dearest. Set a fixed limit on your weekly spending, and make sure you stick to it.

UNDER AGE PLAYING

Compulsive gambling, in any form, is a serious problem. It is vitally important that impressionable youngsters are not introduced to gambling, and should not even be allowed to play the lotto game.

The small minority of lottery retailers who tolerate under age playing do not do themselves any favours. Not only do they risk being prosecuted, and losing their lottery licenses, but they also corrupt the game in the long-term. However, although lottery retailers are in the forefront to curb under age playing, it is the parents who have the responsibility to educate, and supervise their children.

APPENDIX A

CALCULATION OF COMBINATIONS

The number of combinations, with r numbers in each, that can be drawn from a total of n numbers is:

$$\binom{n}{r} = \frac{n!}{r! \times (n-r)!}.$$

In this formula, the exclamation mark means that a number is multiplied by all of its consecutive smaller numbers down to one. For instance, 6!= 1x2x3x4x5x6=720. There is also a special rule: 0!=1.

As an example, the number of six-number combinations that can be drawn from 49 numbers is:

$$\binom{49}{6} = \frac{49!}{6! \times 43!} = \frac{43! \times 44 \times 45 \times 46 \times 47 \times 48 \times 49}{6! \times 43!}$$

$$= 13{,}983{,}816 \sim 14 \text{ million}$$

APPENDIX B

CALCULATION OF WINNING CHANCES

The probability (p) of having a certain amount of correct numbers in a lotto draw can be calculated from the formula:

$$p_q = \frac{\binom{n-r}{r-q} \times \binom{r}{q}}{\binom{n}{r}},$$

where n is the total number of options, r is the amount of numbers drawn and q is the amount of correct numbers. The first term in the numerator represents the incorrect choices and the second term the correct ones. In our 6/49 reference game n=49 and r=6.

6 CORRECT NUMBERS. In Appendix A, we already calculated the total number of six-number combinations that can be drawn in a 6/49 game - 13,983,816. As here q=6, the numerator in the formula becomes one and, thus, the chances of winning are one in ~14 million.

5 CORRECT NUMBERS. Now q=5 and there are

$$\binom{49-6}{6-5}=\binom{43}{1}=\frac{43!}{1!\times 42!}=43$$

ways to choose an incorrect number and

$$\binom{6}{6-1}=\binom{6}{5}=\frac{6!}{5!\times 1!}=6$$

ways to choose correct numbers. The probability of a combination with five correct numbers is then:

$$p_5=\frac{\binom{43}{1}\times\binom{6}{5}}{\binom{49}{6}}=\frac{43\times 6}{13{,}983{,}816}=\frac{1}{54{,}201}.$$

4 CORRECT NUMBERS. Now q=4 and the probability of a combination with four correct numbers is:

$$p_4=\frac{\binom{43}{2}\times\binom{6}{4}}{\binom{49}{6}}=\frac{1}{1{,}032}.$$

3 CORRECT NUMBERS. Now q=3 and the probability of a combination with three correct numbers is:

$$p_3 = \frac{\binom{43}{3} \times \binom{6}{3}}{\binom{49}{6}} = \frac{1}{56.7}$$

5 CORRECT NUMBERS AND A BONUS NUMBER. When there is a bonus number in the game, it can be included in the calculation by imagining that another draw takes place. In our reference game n=43, r=1 and q=1. Even without resorting to the use of the formula for probability, we can see that the chances of having the correct bonus number are one in 43. If there is more than one bonus number in your lotto game, apply the formula as before. Thus, the probability of a combination with five correct numbers plus the bonus number is:

$$p_{5+bonus} = p_5 \times p_{bonus} = \frac{1}{2,330,636}.$$

3 OR MORE CORRECT NUMBERS. To win any prize, the probability is simply the sum of all individual probabilities:

$$p_{any} = p_3 + p_4 + p_5 + p_{5+bonus} + p_6 = \frac{1}{53.7}.$$

The **odds** of a draw with probability p occurring are defined by the ratio:

$$\frac{p}{(1-p)}.$$

This gives, for example, the odds of winning any prize in the 6/49 game as 1 to 52.7.

APPENDIX C

LOTTERY SYSTEMS

Wheeling

To produce all the combinations from a set of more than six numbers, any approach will do as long as it is systematic. Nevertheless **wheeling**, a method separately accredited to mathematicians Dmitrov and Serotic, makes generating combinations easier. Using this method, one or more numbers are eliminated systematically across the board (wheeled) which contains the selected numbers in identical rows. Say, there is a set of any seven numbers labelled 1-7:

I	II	III	IV	V	VI	VII
1	2	3	4	5	6	7

Leaving out one number consecutively in each row produces the seven entries of the full system:

	I	II	III	IV	V	VI	VII
entry1		2	3	4	5	6	7
entry2	1		3	4	5	6	7
entry3	1	2		4	5	6	7
entry4	1	2	3		5	6	7
entry5	1	2	3	4		6	7
entry6	1	2	3	4	5		7
entry7	1	2	3	4	5	6	

For a set of eight numbers, labelled 1-8, the 28 combinations are:

	I	II	III	IV	V	VI	VII	VIII
entry1			3	4	5	6	7	8
entry2		2		4	5	6	7	8
entry3		2	3		5	6	7	8
entry4		2	3	4		6	7	8
entry5		2	3	4	5		7	8
entry6		2	3	4	5	6		8
entry7		2	3	4	5	6	7	
entry8	1			4	5	6	7	8
entry9	1		3		5	6	7	8
entry10	1		3	4		6	7	8
entry11	1		3	4	5		7	8
entry12	1		3	4	5	6		8
entry13	1		3	4	5	6	7	
entry14	1	2			5	6	7	8
entry15	1	2		4		6	7	8
entry16	1	2		4	5		7	8
entry17	1	2		4	5	6		8
entry18	1	2		4	5	6	7	
entry19	1	2	3			6	7	8
entry20	1	2	3		5		7	8
entry21	1	2	3		5	6		8
entry22	1	2	3		5	6	7	
entry23	1	2	3	4			7	8
entry24	1	2	3	4		6		8
entry25	1	2	3	4		6	7	
entry26	1	2	3	4	5			8
entry27	1	2	3	4	5		7	
entry28	1	2	3	4	5	6		

Short wheels

If there are special or lucky numbers in your set, a short wheel can be generated by including only those entries from the full wheel that contain the special numbers. A short wheel can also be obtained by wheeling more than one number at a time. The width of the wheel depends on the size of the set, i.e. two numbers for a set of eight, three for a set of nine, etc. For example, a set of eight numbers would produce, using a two-number wheel, seven entries:

	I	II	III	IV	V	VI	VII	VIII
entry1			3	4	5	6	7	8
entry2	1			4	5	6	7	8
entry3	1	2			5	6	7	8
entry4	1	2	3			6	7	8
entry5	1	2	3	4			7	8
entry6	1	2	3	4	5			8
entry7	1	2	3	4	5	6		

or just four entries:

	I	II	III	IV	V	VI	VII	VIII
entry1			3	4	5	6	7	8
entry2	1	2			5	6	7	8
entry3	1	2	3	4			7	8
entry4	1	2	3	4	5	6		

INDEX